Allergy Free

Recipes and Practical Advice for your Health

General Editor: Gina Steer

FLAME TREE
PUBLISHING

Publisher & Creative Director: Nick Wells
Project Editor: Sarah Goulding
Designer: Mike Spender
With thanks to: Gina Steer

This is a **FLAME TREE** Book

FLAME TREE PUBLISHING
Crabtree Hall, Crabtree Lane
Fulham, London SW6 6TY
United Kingdom
www.flametreepublishing.com

Flame Tree is part of The Foundry Creative Media Company Limited

First published 2005

05 07 09 08 06
1 3 5 7 9 10 8 6 4 2

ISBN 1 84451 114 6

A copy of the CIP data for this book is available from the British Library.

Printed in Malaysia

Contents

Living with Food Allergies

More and more people seem to be suffering from all kinds of allergies, many of which are food and drink related. A food allergy is a reaction from the immune system to a food that the body mistakenly thinks is harmful. The immune system then creates specific antibodies to it, which means that the next time you eat that food the immune system releases massive amounts of chemicals, including histamine, in order to protect the body. These chemicals trigger a range of unpleasant symptoms, which can include nausea, breathing problems, rashes and skin irritation, headaches which can quickly become migraines, cramps and an upset stomach. The food involved can be any food or even a combination of foods, and if you suspect that you have an allergy or food intolerance it is important that you get this investigated so that you can eliminate it from your diet and improve your quality of life.

It is worth bearing in mind that there are varying degrees of allergies, and in some cases the problem is not an allergy but a food intolerance. Food intolerance is a general term that is applied to all reactions that occur after consuming food and drink and can be triggered not necessarily by the food, but by additives that have been artificially added – food colours, pesticides or fertilizers, preservatives and flavourings. Food allergies, on the other hand, are when the body's immune system has an abnormal and violent reaction to a particular food or additive. Food allergies can be triggered by any foods, such as fruits, vegetables and meats, but 90 per cent of reactions are caused by milk, eggs, peanuts, tree nuts (walnuts, cashews, etc.), fish, shellfish, soy and wheat. Reactions to these foods can be very extreme, and similar to how some people react to a bee or wasp sting. This is known as anaphylaxis and can be life threatening. People who are at risk of this should carry an antidote which can be administered immediately and carry a card stating their allergy reaction.

Recent research suggests that one in six people are affected by food allergies, so if you suspect you may be one of them you should see your doctor as soon as possible. If necessary they will refer you to a nutritionist. As well as skin testing, hair analysis and blood tests, a nutritionist may ask you to do an elimination trial in order to pinpoint the problem food groups. This involves eliminating certain foods over a period of time and then gradually re-introducing them to the diet. Once you have worked out which foods present a problem, you should be able to avoid them and thereby improve your well-being and quality of life dramatically.

If a member of your family has a food allergy, it does not necessarily mean you will also be at risk – a food that one person has a problem with can be completely harmless to another member of the same family. Recent research has also shown that food intolerance and allergies can be caused by an enzyme deficiency which can make a particular food difficult to digest. A good example of this is lactose intolerance, which can affect very young babies. Some allergies can be outgrown, however, so a diagnosis of intolerance is not necessarily a life sentence.

If you're suffering from a food allergy, the first and most important step is to look at your diet, but be sure to seek professional advice as described previously before attempting a food elimination experiment. This will ensure that a balanced diet is maintained and a suitable substitute can be introduced if important foods are excluded. Some of the most common allergens are listed below.

Nuts, especially peanuts are one of the biggest culprits especially in young children. It is recommended that all nuts and products that contain nuts are not given to children under the age of five. Many convenience foods, from biscuits, cakes, desserts and ice cream to ready-meals and savoury products may contain nuts, or have been prepared on the same equipment as food containing nuts. Most are now clearly labelled, so checking the ingredient list is vital. Coconut, nutmeg and water chestnuts do not need to be avoided, however.

Cows' milk can also set up an allergic reaction – in this case the intestines cannot tolerate the lactose contained in the milk. Goats' milk protein is similar to that in cows' milk, so is not necessarily a safe alternative. Some people find they cannot digest full cream cows' milk but can tolerate in small amounts skimmed milk, so do not rule cows' milk out altogether until you have investigated this. An adverse reaction to cows' milk normally indicates that cheese, butter, yogurt and cream can also cause problems.

Egg whites can cause allergic reactions, and as eggs are in many products it is vital to read ingredient lists carefully. Toddlers normally seem to be the age group most likely to be affected by an allergy to eggs, but the good news is that they are likely to outgrow this particular intolerance.

Gluten intolerance seems to be increasing rapidly. The major grains that contain gluten are wheat, rye, oats and barley. These grains and their by-products must be strictly avoided by people with a gluten allergy, although wheat-allergic people need only avoid wheat. Rice flour, potato flour or cornflour are good substitutes for wheat flour in any recipe.

Berries such as strawberries and raspberries can cause a reaction, often swelling of the mouth. For some, kiwi fruits, citrus fruits and vegetables such as celery can also be a problem.

Soya beans can also cause a severe allergic reaction. Unfortunately they have become a major part of processed food products, so avoiding them can be difficult as well as possibly resulting in an unbalanced diet. They can be found in baked goods, canned tuna, cereals, crackers, infant formulas, sauces and soups, so always read the label.

Fish and shellfish are a common cause of allergic reactions in both adults and children. It is generally recommended that those who have had an allergic reaction to one species of fish avoid all fish, and the same goes for shellfish. Be aware that Worcestershire sauce often contains anchovies, as do Caesar salad dressings.

This book contains many delicious recipes to help those living with an allergy or food intolerance. It is important to note, however, that whilst we have tried to eliminate or substitute the most obvious causes of allergic reactions, there may still be ingredients that disagree with certain people. Please therefore read the recipe very carefully before cooking, and leave out anything that you think might cause a problem. But with tasty dishes such as Chicken & Summer Vegetable Risotto and Fillet Steaks with Tomato & Garlic Sauce, there should be something for everyone.

Braised Rabbit with Red Peppers

Nutritional details

per 100 g

energy	105 kcals/440 kj
protein	10 g
carbohydrate	4 g
fat	6 g
fibre	0.7 g
sugar	3 g
sodium	0.04 g

Ingredients Serves 4

1.1 kg/2½ lb rabbit pieces
125 ml/¼ fl oz olive oil
grated zest and juice of 1 lemon
2–3 tbsp freshly chopped thyme
salt and freshly ground black pepper
1 onion, peeled and thinly sliced
4 red peppers, deseeded and cut into 2.5 cm/1 inch pieces
2 garlic cloves, peeled and crushed
400 g can strained, crushed tomatoes
1 tsp brown sugar
freshly cooked polenta or creamy mashed potatoes, to serve

Step-by-step guide

1 Place the rabbit pieces in a shallow dish with half the olive oil, the lemon zest and juice, thyme, and some black pepper. Turn until well coated, then cover and leave to marinate for about 1 hour.

2 Heat half the remaining oil in a large, heavy-based casserole dish, add the onion and cook for 5 minutes, then add the peppers and cook for a further 12–15 minutes, or until softened, stirring occasionally. Stir in the garlic, crushed tomatoes and brown sugar and cook, covered, until soft, stirring occasionally.

3 Heat the remaining oil in a large frying pan, drain the rabbit, reserving the marinade, and pat the rabbit dry with absorbent kitchen paper. Add the rabbit to the pan and cook on all sides until golden. Transfer the rabbit to the casserole dish and mix to cover with the tomato sauce.

4 Add the reserved marinade to the frying pan, stirring to loosen any browned bits from the pan. Add to the rabbit and stir gently.

5 Cover the pan and simmer for 30 minutes or until the rabbit is tender. Serve the rabbit and the vegetable mixture on a bed of polenta or creamy mashed potatoes.

✓ cows' milk-free ✓ egg-free ✓ gluten-free ✓ wheat-free ✓ nut-free ✓ vegetarian ✓ vegan ✓ seafood-free

Cawl

Nutritional details

per 100 g

energy	210 kcals/868 kj
protein	6 g
carbohydrate	5 g
fat	19 g
fibre	1 g
sugar	1 g
sodium	0.09 g

Ingredients Serves 4–6

700 g/1½ lb scrag end of lamb or best end of neck chops
pinch of salt
2 large onions, peeled and thinly sliced
3 large potatoes, peeled and cut into chunks
2 parsnips, peeled and cut into chunks
1 swede, peeled and cut into chunks
3 large carrots, peeled and cut into chunks
2 leeks, trimmed and sliced
freshly ground black pepper
4 tbsp freshly chopped parsley

Step-by-step guide

1 Put the lamb in a large saucepan, cover with cold water and bring to the boil. Add a generous pinch of salt. Simmer gently for 1½ hours, then set aside to cool completely, preferably overnight.

2 The next day, skim the fat off the surface of the lamb liquid and discard. Return the saucepan to the heat and bring back to the boil. Simmer for 5 minutes. Add the onions, potatoes, parsnips, swede and carrots and return to the boil. Reduce the heat, cover and cook for about 20 minutes, stirring occasionally.

3 Add the leeks and season to taste with salt and pepper. Cook for a further 10 minutes, or until all the vegetables are tender.

4 Using a slotted spoon, remove the meat from the saucepan and take the meat off the bone. Discard the bones and any gristle, then return the meat to the pan. Adjust the seasoning to taste, stir in the parsley, then serve immediately.

Chicken & Summer Vegetable Risotto

Nutritional details

per 100 g

energy	194 kcals/808 kj
protein	14 g
carbohydrate	18 g
fat	6 g
fibre	2 g
sugar	0.8 g
sodium	0.6 g

Ingredients Serves 4

1 litre/1¾ pint gluten-free chicken or vegetable stock
225 g/8 oz baby asparagus spears
125 g/4 oz French beans
2 tsp olive oil
1 small onion, peeled and finely chopped
150 ml/¼ pint dry white wine
275 g/10 oz arborio rice
pinch of saffron strands
75 g/3 oz frozen peas, thawed
225 g/8 oz cooked chicken, skinned and diced
juice of ½ lemon
salt and freshly ground black pepper

Step-by-step guide

1 Bring the stock to the boil in a large saucepan. Trim the asparagus and cut into 4 cm/1½ inch lengths.

2 Blanch the asparagus in the stock for 1–2 minutes or until tender, then remove with a slotted spoon and reserve.

3 Halve the green beans and cook in the boiling stock for 4 minutes. Remove and reserve. Turn down the heat and keep the stock barely simmering.

4 Heat the oil in a heavy-based saucepan. Add the onion and cook gently for about 5 minutes.

5 Pour the wine into the pan and boil rapidly until the liquid has almost reduced. Add the rice and cook, stirring for 1 minute until the grains are coated and look translucent.

6 Add the saffron and a ladle of the stock. Simmer, stirring all the time, until the stock has absorbed. Continue adding the stock, a ladle at a time, until it has all been absorbed.

7 After 15 minutes the risotto should be creamy with a slight bite to it. If not add a little more stock and cook for a few more minutes, or until it is of the correct texture and consistency.

8 Add the peas, reserved vegetables, chicken and lemon juice. Season to taste with salt and pepper and cook for 3–4 minutes or until the chicken is thoroughly heated and piping hot.

9 Spoon the risotto on to warmed serving plates and serve immediately.

✓ cows' milk-free ✓ egg-free ✓ gluten-free ✓ wheat-free ✓ nut-free ✓ vegetarian ✓ vegan ✓ seafood-free

Chicken with Roasted Fennel & Citrus Rice

Nutritional details

per 100 g

energy	108 kcals/450 kj
protein	9 g
carbohydrate	8 g
fat	5 g
fibre	0.3 g
sugar	0.8 g
sodium	0.2 g

Ingredients Serves 4

2 tsp fennel seeds
1 tbsp freshly chopped oregano
1 garlic clove, peeled and crushed
salt and freshly ground black pepper
4 chicken quarters, about 175 g/6 oz each
½ lemon, finely sliced
1 fennel bulb, trimmed
2 tsp olive oil
4 plum tomatoes
25 g/1 oz stoned green olives

To garnish:
fennel fronds,orange slices

For the citrus rice:
225 g/8 oz long-grain rice
finely grated rind and juice of ½ lemon
150 ml/¼ pint orange juice
450 ml/¾ pint boiling gluten-free chicken or vegetable stock

Step-by-step guide

1 Preheat the oven to 200°C/400°F/Gas Mark 6. Lightly crush the fennel seeds and mix with oregano, garlic, salt and pepper. Place between the skin and flesh of the chicken breasts, being careful not to tear the skin. Arrange the lemon slices on top of the chicken.

2 Cut the fennel into eight wedges. Place on baking tray with the chicken. Lightly brush the fennel with the oil. Cook the chicken and fennel on the top shelf of the preheated oven for 10 minutes.

3 Meanwhile, put the rice in a 2.3 litre/4 pint ovenproof dish. Stir in the lemon rind and juice, orange juice and stock. Cover with a lid and put on the middle shelf of the oven.

4 Reduce the oven temperature to 180°C/350°F/Gas Mark 4. Cook the chicken for a further 40 minutes, turning the fennel wedges and lemon slices once. Deseed and chop the tomatoes. Add to the tray and cook for 5–10 minutes. Remove from the oven.

5 When cooled slightly, remove the chicken skin and discard. Fluff the rice, scatter olives over the dish, garnish with the fennel fronds and orange slices and serve.

Chilli Roast Chicken

Nutritional details

per 100 g

energy	168 kcals/704 kj
protein	16 g
carbohydrate	4 g
fat	10 g
fibre	0.02 g
sugar	0.02 g
sodium	0.1 g

Ingredients — Serves 4

3 medium-hot fresh red chillies, deseeded
½ tsp ground turmeric
1 tsp cumin seeds
1 tsp coriander seeds
2 garlic cloves, peeled and crushed
2.5 cm/1 inch piece fresh root ginger, peeled and chopped
1 tbsp lemon juice
1 tbsp olive oil
2 tbsp roughly chopped fresh coriander
½ tsp salt
freshly ground black pepper
1.4 kg/3 lb oven-ready chicken
15 g/½ oz dairy-free margarine, melted
550 g/1¼ lb butternut squash
fresh parsley and coriander sprigs, to garnish

To serve:
4 baked potatoes
seasonal green vegetables

Step-by-step guide

1. Preheat the oven to 190°C/375°F/Gas Mark 5. Roughly chop the chillies and put in a food processor with the turmeric, cumin seeds, coriander seeds, garlic, ginger, lemon juice, olive oil, coriander, salt, pepper and 2 tablespoons of cold water. Blend to a paste, leaving the ingredients still slightly chunky.

2. Starting at the neck end of the chicken, gently ease up the skin to loosen it from the breast. Reserve 3 tablespoons of the paste. Push the remaining paste over the chicken breast under the skin, spreading it evenly.

3. Put the chicken in a large roasting tin. Mix the reserved chilli paste with the melted margarine. Brush 1 tablespoon of it evenly over the chicken and roast in the preheated oven for 20 minutes.

4. Meanwhile, halve, peel and scoop out the seeds from the butternut squash. Cut into large chunks and mix in the remaining chilli paste and margarine mixture.

5. Arrange the butternut squash around the chicken. Roast for a further hour, basting with the cooking juices about every 20 minutes until the chicken is fully cooked and the squash tender. Garnish with parsley and coriander. Serve hot with baked potatoes and green vegetables.

✓ cows' milk-free ✓ egg-free ✓ gluten-free ✓ wheat-free ✓ nut-free ✓ vegetarian ✓ vegan ✓ seafood-free

Chinese-glazed Poussin with Green & Black Rice

Nutritional details

per 100 g

energy	178 kcals/744 kj
protein	17 g
carbohydrate	6 g
fat	9 g
fibre	0.2 g
sugar	2 g
sodium	0.08 g

Ingredients Serves 4

4 oven-ready poussins
salt and freshly ground black pepper
300 ml/½ pint apple juice
1 cinnamon stick
2 star anise
½ tsp Chinese five spice powder
50 g/2 oz dark muscovado sugar
2 tbsp tomato purée
1 tbsp cider vinegar
grated rind of 1 orange
350 g/12 oz mixed basmati and wild rice
125 g/4 oz mangetout, finely sliced lengthways
1 bunch spring onions, trimmed and finely shredded lengthways
salt and freshly ground black pepper

Step-by-step guide

1. Preheat the oven to 200°C/400°F/Gas Mark 6, 15 minutes before cooking. Rinse the poussins inside and out and pat dry with absorbent kitchen paper. Using tweezers, remove any feathers. Season well with salt and pepper, then reserve.

2. Pour the apple juice into a small saucepan and add the cinnamon stick, star anise and Chinese five spice powder. Bring to the boil, then simmer rapidly until reduced by half. Reduce the heat, stir in the sugar, tomato purée, vinegar and orange rind and simmer gently until the sugar is dissolved and the glaze is syrupy. Remove from the heat and leave to cool completely. Remove the whole spices.

3. Place the poussins on a wire rack set over a tinfoil-lined roasting tin. Brush generously with the apple glaze. Roast in the preheated oven for 40–45 minutes, or until the juices run clear when the thigh is pierced with a skewer, basting once or twice with the remaining glaze. Remove the poussins from the oven and leave to cool slightly.

4. Meanwhile, cook the rice according to the packet instructions. Bring a large saucepan of lightly salted water to the boil and add the mangetout. Blanch for 1 minute, then drain thoroughly. As soon as the rice is cooked, drain and transfer to a warmed bowl. Add the mangetout and spring onions, season to taste and stir well. Arrange on warmed dinner plates, place a poussin on top and serve immediately.

cows' milk-free · egg-free · gluten-free · wheat-free · nut-free · vegetarian · vegan · seafood-free

Chinese Leaf & Mushroom Soup

Nutritional details

per 100 g

energy	72 kcals/297 kj
protein	4 g
carbohydrate	4 g
fat	5 g
fibre	0.09 g
sugar	0.6 g
sodium	0.55 g

Ingredients Serves 4–6

450 g/1 lb Chinese leaves
25 g/1 oz dried Chinese (shiitake) mushrooms
1 tbsp vegetable oil
75 g/3 oz smoked streaky bacon, diced
2.5 cm/1 inch piece fresh root ginger, peeled and finely chopped
175 g/6 oz chestnut mushrooms, thinly sliced
1.1 litres/2 pints gluten-free chicken stock
4–6 spring onions, trimmed and cut into short lengths
2 tbsp dry sherry or Chinese rice wine
salt and freshly ground black pepper
sesame oil for drizzling

Step-by-step guide

1 Trim the stem ends of the Chinese leaves and cut in half lengthways. Remove the triangular core with a knife, then cut into 2.5 cm/1 inch slices and reserve.

2 Place the dried Chinese mushrooms in a bowl and pour over enough almost-boiling water to cover. Leave to stand for 20 minutes to soften, then gently lift out and squeeze out the liquid. Discard the stems and thinly slice the caps and reserve. Strain the liquid through a muslin-lined sieve or a coffee filter paper and reserve.

3 Heat a wok over a medium-high heat, add the oil and when hot add the bacon. Stir-fry for 3–4 minutes, or until crisp and golden, stirring frequently. Add the ginger and chestnut mushrooms and stir-fry for a further 2–3 minutes.

4 Add the chicken stock and bring to the boil, skimming off any fat and scum that rises to the surface. Add the spring onions, sherry or rice wine, Chinese leaves, sliced Chinese mushrooms and season to taste with salt and pepper. Pour in the reserved soaking liquid and reduce the heat to the lowest possible setting.

5 Simmer gently, covered, until all the vegetables are very tender; this will take about 10 minutes. Add a little water if the liquid has reduced too much. Spoon into soup bowls and drizzle with a little sesame oil. Serve immediately.

cows' milk-free · egg-free · gluten-free · wheat-free · nut-free · vegetarian · vegan · seafood-free

Coconut-baked Courgettes

Nutritional details

per 100 g

energy	112 kcals/468 kj
protein	3 g
carbohydrate	4 g
fat	10 g
fibre	2 g
sugar	3 g
sodium	trace

Ingredients　Serves 4

3 tbsp sunflower oil
1 onion, peeled and finely sliced
4 garlic cloves, peeled and crushed
½ tsp chilli powder
1 tsp ground coriander
6–8 tbsp desiccated coconut
1 tbsp tomato purée
700 g/1½ lb courgettes, thinly sliced
freshly chopped parsley, to garnish

Step-by-step guide

1 Preheat the oven to 180°C/350°F/ Gas Mark 4, 10 minutes before cooking. Lightly oil a 1.4 litre/ 2½ pint ovenproof gratin dish. Heat a wok, add the oil and when hot, add the onion and stir-fry for 2–3 minutes. Add the garlic, chilli powder and coriander and stir-fry for 1–2 minutes.

2 Pour 300 ml/½ pint cold water into the wok and bring to the boil. Add the coconut and tomato purée and simmer for 3–4 minutes; most of the water will evaporate at this stage. Spoon 4 tablespoons of the spice and coconut mixture into a small bowl and reserve.

3 Stir the courgettes into the remaining spice and coconut mixture and spoon into the oiled gratin dish. Sprinkle the reserved spice and coconut mixture evenly over the top. Bake, uncovered, in the preheated oven for 15–20 minutes, or until golden. Garnish with chopped parsley and serve. **Please note that coconut is fine for most nut allergy sufferers, but please check with your doctor if you have any concerns.**

Coconut Beef

Nutritional details

per 100 g

energy	243 kcals/1013 kj
protein	13 g
carbohydrate	12 g
fat	17 g
fibre	0.2 g
sugar	1 g
sodium	0.1 g

Step-by-step guide

1 Trim off any fat or gristle from the beef and cut into thin strips. Heat a wok or large frying pan, add 2 tablespoons of the oil and heat until just smoking. Add the beef and cook for 5–8 minutes, turning occasionally, until browned on all sides. Using a slotted spoon, transfer the beef to a plate and keep warm.

2 Add the remaining oil to the wok and heat until almost smoking. Add the spring onions, chilli, garlic and ginger and cook for 1 minute, stirring occasionally. Add the mushrooms and stir-fry for 3 minutes. Using a slotted spoon, transfer the mushroom mixture to a plate and keep warm.

3 Return the beef to the wok and pour in the coconut cream and stock. Bring to the boil and simmer for 3–4 minutes, or until the juices are slightly reduced and the beef is just tender.

4 Return the mushroom mixture to the wok and heat through. Stir in the chopped coriander and season to taste with salt and pepper. Serve immediately with freshly cooked rice. **See note on page 13.**

Ingredients Serves 4

450 g/1 lb beef rump or sirloin steak
4 tbsp sunflower oil
2 bunches spring onions, trimmed and thickly sliced
1 red chilli, deseeded and chopped
1 garlic clove, peeled and chopped
2 cm/1 inch piece fresh root ginger, peeled and cut into matchsticks
125 g/4 oz shiitake mushrooms
200 ml/7 fl oz coconut cream
150 ml/¼ pint chicken stock
4 tbsp freshly chopped coriander
salt and freshly ground black pepper
freshly cooked rice, to serve

cows' milk-free · egg-free · gluten-free · wheat-free · nut-free · vegetarian · vegan · seafood-free

Coconut Chicken Soup

Nutritional details

per 100 g

energy	121 kcals/510 kj
protein	7 g
carbohydrate	14 g
fat	4 g
fibre	0.7 g
sugar	4.1 g
sodium	0.2 g

Ingredients Serves 4

2 lemon grass stalks
3 tbsp vegetable oil
3 medium onions, peeled and finely sliced
3 garlic cloves, peeled and crushed
2 tbsp fresh root ginger, finely grated
2–3 kaffir lime leaves
1½ tsp turmeric
1 red pepper, deseeded and diced
400 ml can coconut milk
1.1 litres/2 pints gluten-free vegetable or chicken stock
275 g/9 oz easy-cook long-grain rice
275 g/10 oz cooked chicken meat
285 g can sweetcorn, drained
3 tbsp freshly chopped coriander
freshly chopped pickled chillies, to serve

Step-by-step guide

1 Discard the outer leaves of the lemon grass stalks, then place on a chopping board and, using a mallet or rolling pin, pound gently to bruise; reserve.

2 Heat the vegetable oil in a large saucepan and cook the onions over a medium heat for about 10–15 minutes until soft and beginning to change colour.

3 Lower the heat, stir in the garlic, ginger, lime leaves and turmeric and cook for 1 minute. Add the red pepper, coconut milk, stock, lemon grass and rice. Bring to the boil, cover and simmer gently over a low heat for about 10 minutes.

4 Cut the chicken into bite-sized pieces, then stir into the soup, with the sweetcorn and the freshly chopped coriander. Reheat gently, stirring frequently. Serve immediately with a few chopped pickled chillies to sprinkle on top. **See note on page 13.**

✓ cows' milk-free ✓ egg-free ✓ gluten-free ✓ wheat-free ✓ nut-free ✓ vegetarian ✓ vegan ✓ seafood-free

Duck with Berry Sauce

Nutritional details

per 100 g

energy	119 kcals/502 kj
protein	10 g
carbohydrate	9 g
fat	5 g
fibre	0.8 g
sugar	4 g
sodium	trace

Ingredients Serves 4

4 x 175 g/6 oz boneless duck breasts
salt and freshly ground black pepper
1 tsp sunflower oil

For the sauce:
juice of 1 orange
1 bay leaf
3 tbsp redcurrant jelly
150 g/5 oz fresh or frozen mixed berries
2 tbsp dried cranberries or cherries
½ tsp soft light brown sugar
1 tbsp balsamic vinegar
1 tsp freshly chopped mint
sprigs of fresh mint, to garnish

To serve:
freshly cooked potatoes
freshly cooked green beans

Step-by-step guide

1 Remove the skins from the duck breasts and season with a little salt and pepper. Brush a griddle pan with the oil, then heat on the stove until smoking hot.

2 Place the duck, skinned-side down in the pan. Cook over a medium-high heat for 5 minutes, or until well browned. Turn the duck and cook for 2 minutes. Lower the heat and cook for a further 5–8 minutes, or until cooked, but still slightly pink in the centre. Remove from the pan and keep warm.

3 While the duck is cooking, make the sauce. Put the orange juice, bay leaf, redcurrant jelly, fresh or frozen and dried berries and sugar in a small griddle pan. Add any juices left in the griddle pan to the small pan. Slowly bring to the boil, lower the heat and simmer uncovered for 4–5 minutes, until the fruit is soft.

4 Remove the bay leaf. Stir in the vinegar and chopped mint and season to taste with salt and pepper.

5 Slice the duck breasts on the diagonal and arrange on serving plates. Spoon over the berry sauce and garnish with sprigs of fresh mint. Serve immediately with the potatoes and green beans.

cows' milk-free · egg-free · gluten-free · wheat-free · nut-free · vegetarian · vegan · seafood-free

Fillet Steaks with Tomato & Garlic Sauce

Nutritional details

per 100 g

energy	142 kcals/594 kj
protein	15 g
carbohydrate	7 g
fat	6 g
fibre	0.2 g
sugar	trace
sodium	0.4 g

Ingredients — Serves 4

- 700 g/1½ lb ripe tomatoes
- 2 garlic cloves
- 2 tbsp olive oil
- 2 tbsp freshly chopped basil
- 2 tbsp freshly chopped oregano
- 2 tbsp red wine
- salt and freshly ground black pepper
- 75 g/3 oz pitted black olives, chopped
- 4 fillet steaks, about 175 g/6 oz each in weight
- freshly cooked vegetables, to serve

Step-by-step guide

1. Make a small cross on the top of each tomato and place in a large bowl. Cover with boiling water and leave for 2 minutes. Using a slotted spoon, remove the tomatoes and skin carefully. Repeat until all the tomatoes are skinned. Place on a chopping board, cut into quarters, remove the seeds and roughly chop, then reserve.

2. Peel and chop the garlic. Heat half the olive oil in a saucepan and cook the garlic for 30 seconds. Add the chopped tomatoes with the basil, oregano, red wine and season to taste with salt and pepper. Bring to the boil then reduce the heat, cover and simmer for 15 minutes, stirring occasionally, or until the sauce is reduced and thickened. Stir the olives into the sauce and keep warm while cooking the steaks.

3. Meanwhile, lightly oil a griddle pan or heavy-based frying pan with the remaining olive oil and cook the steaks for 2 minutes on each side to seal. Continue to cook the steaks for a further 2–4 minutes, depending on personal preference. Serve the steaks immediately with the garlic sauce and freshly cooked vegetables.

✓ cows' milk-free ✓ egg-free ✓ gluten-free ✓ wheat-free ✓ nut-free ✓ vegetarian ✓ vegan ✓ seafood-free

Fried Rice with Bamboo Shoots & Ginger

Nutritional details

per 100 g

energy	92 kcals/381 kj
protein	2 g
carbohydrate	10 g
fat	5 g
fibre	0.5 g
sugar	0.7 g
sodium	0.2 g

  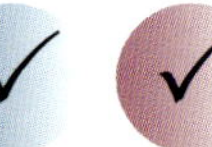

Ingredients Serves 4

4 tbsp sunflower oil
1 onion, peeled and finely chopped
225 g/8 oz long-grain rice
3 garlic cloves, peeled and cut into slivers
2.5 cm/1 inch piece fresh root ginger, peeled and grated
3 spring onions, trimmed and chopped
450 ml/¾ pint gluten-free vegetable stock
125 g/4 oz button mushrooms, wiped and halved
75 g/3 oz frozen peas, thawed
500 g can bamboo shoots, drained and thinly sliced
salt and freshly ground black pepper
fresh coriander leaves, to garnish

Step-by-step guide

1 Heat a wok, add the oil and when hot, add the onion and cook gently for 3–4 minutes. Add the long-grain rice and cook for 3–4 minutes or until golden, stirring frequently.

2 Add the garlic, ginger and chopped spring onions to the wok and stir well. Pour the chicken stock into a small saucepan and bring to the boil. Carefully ladle the hot stock into the wok, stir well, then simmer gently for 10 minutes or until most of the liquid has been absorbed.

3 Stir the button mushrooms and peas into the wok and continue to cook for a further 5 minutes, or until the rice is tender, adding a little extra stock if necessary.

4 Add the bamboo shoots to the wok and carefully stir in. Season to taste with salt and pepper. Cook for 2–3 minutes or until heated through. Tip on to a warmed serving dish, garnish with coriander leaves and serve immediately.

cows' milk-free · egg-free · gluten-free · wheat-free · nut-free · vegetarian · vegan · seafood-free

Ginger & Garlic Potatoes

Nutritional details

per 100 g

energy	116 kcals/487 kj
protein	2 g
carbohydrate	15 g
fat	6 g
fibre	1 g
sugar	0.7 g
sodium	0.2 g

Step-by-step guide

1 Scrub the potatoes, then place, unpeeled, in a large saucepan and cover with boiling salted water. Bring to the boil and cook for 15 minutes, then drain and leave the potatoes to cool completely. Peel and cut into 2.5 cm/1 inch cubes.

2 Place the root ginger, garlic, turmeric and salt in a food processor and blend for 1 minute. With the motor still running, slowly add 3 tablespoons of water and blend into a paste. Alternatively, pound the ingredients to a paste with a pestle and mortar.

3 Heat the oil in a large heavy-based frying pan and when hot, but not smoking, add the fennel seeds and fry for a few minutes. Stir in the ginger paste and cook for 2 minutes, stirring frequently. Take care not to burn the mixture.

4 Reduce the heat, then add the potatoes and cook for 5–7 minutes, stirring frequently, until the potatoes have a golden-brown crust. Add the diced apple and spring onions, then sprinkle with the freshly chopped coriander. Heat through for 2 minutes, then serve on assorted salad leaves.

Ingredients Serves 4

700 g/1½ lb potatoes
2.5 cm/1 inch piece of root ginger, peeled and coarsely chopped
3 garlic cloves, peeled and chopped
½ tsp turmeric
1 tsp salt
5 tbsp vegetable oil
1 tsp whole fennel seeds
1 large eating apple, cored and diced
6 spring onions, trimmed and sliced diagonally
1 tbsp freshly chopped coriander

To serve:
assorted bitter salad leaves

✓ cows' milk-free ✓ egg-free ✓ gluten-free ✓ wheat-free ✓ nut-free ✓ vegetarian ✓ vegan ✓ seafood-free

Grilled Steaks with Saffron Potatoes & Roast Tomatoes

Nutritional details

per 100 g

energy	118 kcals/493 kj
protein	10 g
carbohydrate	6 g
fat	6 g
fibre	1 g
sugar	2 g
sodium	0.1 g

Ingredients — Serves 4

700 g/1½ lb new potatoes, halved
few strands of saffron
300 ml/½ pint gluten-free vegetable or beef stock
1 small onion, peeled and finely chopped
salt and freshly ground black pepper
2 tsp balsamic vinegar
2 tbsp olive oil, plus 1 tbsp for frying
1 tsp caster sugar
8 plum tomatoes, halved
4 boneless sirloin steaks, each weighing 225 g/8 oz
2 tbsp freshly chopped parsley

Step-by-step guide

1 Cook the potatoes in boiling salted water for 8 minutes and drain well. Return the potatoes to the saucepan along with the saffron, stock and onion. Season to taste with salt and pepper and simmer, uncovered for 10 minutes until the potatoes are tender.

2 Meanwhile, preheat the grill to medium. Mix together the vinegar, 2 tablespoons of olive oil, sugar and seasoning. Arrange the tomatoes cut-side up in a foil-lined grill pan and drizzle over the dressing. Grill for 12–15 minutes, basting occasionally, until tender.

3 Heat the remaining olive oil in a frying pan. Add the steaks and cook for 4–8 minutes to taste and depending on thickness.

4 Arrange the potatoes and tomatoes in the centre of four serving plates. Top with the steaks along with any pan juices. Sprinkle over the parsley and serve immediately.

✓ cows' milk-free ✓ egg-free ✓ gluten-free ✓ wheat-free ✓ nut-free ✓ vegetarian ✓ vegan ✓ seafood-free

Hot-&-Sour Duck

Nutritional details

per 100 g

energy	258 kcals/1078 kj
protein	10 g
carbohydrate	9 g
fat	20 g
fibre	0.1 g
sugar	trace
sodium	0.2 g

Ingredients **Serves 4**

4 small boneless duck breasts, with skin on, thinly sliced on the diagonal
1 tsp salt
4 tbsp tamarind pulp
4 shallots, peeled and chopped
2 garlic cloves, peeled and chopped
2.5 cm/1 inch piece fresh root ginger, chopped
1 tsp ground coriander
3 large red chillies, deseeded and chopped
½ tsp turmeric
125 ml/4 fl oz vegetable oil
227 g can bamboo shoots, drained, rinsed and finely sliced
salt and freshly ground black pepper
sprigs of fresh coriander, to garnish
freshly cooked rice, to serve

Step-by-step guide

1. Sprinkle the duck with the salt, cover lightly and refrigerate for 20 minutes.

2. Meanwhile, place the tamarind pulp in a small bowl, pour over 4 tablespoons of hot water and leave for 2–3 minutes or until softened. Press the mixture through a sieve into another bowl to produce about 2 tablespoons of smooth juice.

3. Place the tamarind juice in a food processor with the shallots, garlic, ginger, coriander, chillies and turmeric. Blend until smooth, adding a little more hot water if necessary, and reserve the paste.

4. Heat a wok or large frying pan, add the oil and when hot, stir-fry the duck in batches for about 3 minutes, or until just coloured, then drain on absorbent kitchen paper.

5. Discard all but 2 tablespoons of the oil in the wok. Return to the heat. Add the paste and stir-fry for 5 minutes. Add the duck and stir-fry for 2 minutes. Add the bamboo shoots and stir-fry for 2 minutes. Season to taste with salt and pepper. Turn into a warmed serving dish, garnish with a sprig of fresh coriander and serve immediately with rice.

Hot & Spicy Red Cabbage with Apples

Nutritional details

per 100 g

energy	42 kcals/176 kj
protein	1 g
carbohydrate	8 g
fat	0.6 g
fibre	0.4 g
sugar	5 g
sodium	trace

Ingredients   Serves 8

900 g/2 lb red cabbage, cored and shredded
450 g/1 lb onions, peeled and finely sliced
450 g/1 lb cooking apples, peeled, cored and finely sliced
½ tsp mixed spice
1 tsp ground cinnamon
2 tbsp light soft brown sugar
salt and freshly ground black pepper
grated rind of 1 large orange
1 tbsp fresh orange juice
50 ml/2 fl oz medium sweet cider (or apple juice)
2 tbsp wine vinegar

To serve:
dairy-free yogurt
freshly ground black pepper

Step-by-step guide

1 Preheat the oven to 150°C/300°F/ Gas Mark 2. Put just enough cabbage in a large casserole dish to cover the base evenly.

2 Place a layer of the onions and apples on top of the cabbage.

3 Sprinkle a little of the mixed spice, cinnamon and sugar over the top. Season with salt and pepper.

4 Spoon over a small portion of the orange rind, orange juice and the cider.

5 Continue to layer the casserole dish with the ingredients in the same order until used up.

6 Pour the vinegar as evenly as possible over the top layer of the ingredients.

7 Cover the casserole dish with a close-fitting lid and bake in the preheated oven, stirring occasionally, for 2 hours until the cabbage is moist and tender. Serve immediately with the dairy-free yogurt and black pepper.

✓ cows' milk-free ✓ egg-free ✓ gluten-free ✓ wheat-free ✓ nut-free ✓ vegetarian ✓ vegan ✓ seafood-free

Lancashire Hotpot

Nutritional details

per 100 g

energy	148 kcals/620 kj
protein	14 g
carbohydrate	8 g
fat	7 g
fibre	0.8 g
sugar	0.5 g
sodium	trace

Ingredients — Serves 4

- 1 kg/2¼ lb middle end neck of lamb, divided into cutlets
- 2 tbsp vegetable oil
- 2 large onions, peeled and sliced
- 2 tsp cornflour
- 150 ml/¼ pint gluten-free vegetable or lamb stock
- 700 g/1½ lb waxy potatoes, peeled and thickly sliced
- salt and freshly ground black pepper
- 1 bay leaf
- 2 sprigs of fresh thyme
- 1 tbsp olive oil
- 2 tbsp freshly chopped herbs, to garnish
- freshly cooked green beans, to serve

Step-by-step guide

1 Preheat the oven to 170°C/325°F/ Gas Mark 3. Trim any excess fat from the lamb cutlets. Heat the oil in a frying pan and brown the cutlets in batches for 3–4 minutes. Remove with a slotted spoon and reserve. Add the onions to the frying pan and cook for 6–8 minutes until softened and just beginning to colour, then remove and reserve.

2 Stir in the cornflour and cook for a few seconds, then gradually pour in the stock, stirring well, and bring to the boil. Remove from the heat.

3 Spread the base of a large casserole with half the potato slices. Top with half the onions and season well with salt and pepper. Arrange the browned meat in a layer. Season again and add the remaining onions, bay leaf and thyme. Pour in the remaining liquid from the onions and top with the remaining potatoes so that they overlap in a single layer. Brush the potatoes with the melted butter and season again.

4 Cover the saucepan and cook in the oven for 2 hours, uncovering for the last 30 minutes to brown the top. Garnish with chopped herbs and serve with green beans.

cows' milk-free · egg-free · gluten-free · wheat-free · nut-free · vegetarian · vegan · seafood-free

Leek & Ham Risotto

Nutritional details

per 100 g

energy	86 kcals/358 kj
protein	5 g
carbohydrate	11 g
fat	3 g
fibre	0.6 g
sugar	0.2 g
sodium	0.4 g

Ingredients — Serves 4

1 tbsp olive oil
1 medium onion, peeled and finely chopped
4 leeks, trimmed and thinly sliced
1½ tbsp freshly chopped thyme
350 g/12 oz Arborio rice
1.4 litres/2¼ pints gluten-free vegetable or chicken stock, heated
225 g/8 oz cooked ham
175 g/6 oz peas, thawed if frozen
salt and freshly ground black pepper

Step-by-step guide

1. Heat the oil in a large saucepan. Add the onion and leeks and cook over a medium heat for 6–8 minutes, stirring occasionally, until soft and beginning to colour. Stir in the thyme and cook briefly.
2. Add the rice and stir well. Continue stirring over a medium heat for about 1 minute until the rice is glossy.
3. Add a ladleful or two of the stock and stir well until the stock is absorbed. Continue adding stock, a ladleful at a time, and stirring well between additions, until about two thirds of the stock has been added.
4. Meanwhile, either chop or finely shred the ham, then add to the saucepan of rice together with the peas.
5. Continue adding ladlefuls of stock, as described in step 3, until the rice is tender and the ham is heated through thoroughly.
6. Season to taste with salt and pepper and serve immediately.

✓ cows' milk-free ✓ egg-free ✓ gluten-free ✓ wheat-free ✓ nut-free ✓ vegetarian ✓ vegan ✓ seafood-free

Leg of Lamb with Minted Rice

Nutritional details

per 100 g

energy	174 kcals/729 kj
protein	25 g
carbohydrate	2 g
fat	7 g
fibre	0.1 g
sugar	0.3 g
sodium	0.1 g

Ingredients **Serves 4**

1 tbsp olive oil
1 medium onion, peeled and finely chopped
1 garlic clove, peeled and crushed
1 celery stalk, trimmed and chopped (optional)
1 large mild red chilli, deseeded and chopped
75 g/3 oz long-grain rice
150 ml/¼ pint gluten-free lamb or chicken stock
2 tbsp freshly chopped mint
salt and freshly ground black pepper
1.4 kg/3 lb boned leg of lamb
freshly cooked vegetables, to serve

Step-by-step guide

1 Preheat the oven to 190°C/375°F/Gas Mark 5, 10 minutes before roasting. Heat the oil in a frying pan and cook the onion for 5 minutes. Stir in the garlic, celery (if using) and chilli and continue to cook for 3–4 minutes.

2 Place the rice and the stock in a large saucepan and cook, covered, for 10–12 minutes or until the rice is tender and all the liquid is absorbed. Stir in the onion and celery mixture, then leave to cool. Once the rice mixture is cold, stir in the chopped mint and season to taste with salt and pepper.

3 Place the boned lamb skin-side down and spoon the rice mixture along the centre of the meat. Roll up the meat to enclose the stuffing and tie securely with string. Place in a roasting tin and roast in the preheated oven for 1 hour 20 minutes, or until cooked to personal preference. Remove from the oven and leave to rest in a warm place for 20 minutes, before carving. Serve with a selection of cooked vegetables.

Lemon Chicken with Potatoes, Rosemary & Olives

Nutritional details

per 100 g

energy	158 kcals/660 kj
protein	8 g
carbohydrate	15 g
fat	8 g
fibre	1 g
sugar	1 g
sodium	0.1 g

Ingredients Serves 6

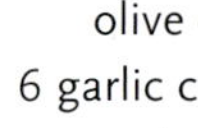

12 skinless boneless chicken thighs
1 large lemon
125 ml/4 fl oz extra virgin olive oil
6 garlic cloves, peeled and sliced
2 onions, peeled and thinly sliced
bunch of fresh rosemary
1.1 kg/2 ½ lb potatoes, peeled and cut into 4 cm/1½ inch pieces
salt and freshly ground black pepper
18–24 black olives, pitted

To serve:
steamed carrots
courgettes

Step-by-step guide

1 Preheat oven to 200°C/400°F/Gas Mark 6, 15 minutes before cooking. Trim the chicken thighs and place in a shallow baking dish large enough to hold them in a single layer. Remove the rind from the lemon with a zester or, if using a peeler, cut into thin julienne strips. Reserve half and add the remainder to the chicken. Squeeze the lemon juice over the chicken, toss to coat well and leave to stand for 10 minutes.

2 Transfer the chicken to a roasting tin. Add the remaining lemon zest or julienne strips, olive oil, garlic, onions and half of the rosemary sprigs. Toss gently and leave for about 20 minutes.

3 Cover the potatoes with lightly salted water and bring to the boil. Cook for 2 minutes, then drain well and add to the chicken. Season to taste with salt and pepper.

4 Roast the chicken in the preheated oven for 50 minutes, turning frequently and basting, or until the chicken is cooked. Just before the end of cooking time, discard the rosemary, and add fresh sprigs of rosemary. Add the olives and stir. Serve immediately with steamed carrots and courgettes.

✓ cows' milk-free ✓ egg-free ✓ gluten-free ✓ wheat-free ✓ nut-free ✓ vegetarian ✓ vegan ✓ seafood-free

Light Ratatouille

Nutritional details

per 100 g

energy	29 kcals/124 kj
protein	1 g
carbohydrate	5 g
fat	0.6 g
fibre	1 g
sugar	2 g
sodium	0.1 g

Ingredients   Serves 4

1 red pepper
2 courgettes, trimmed
1 small aubergine, trimmed
1 onion, peeled
2 ripe tomatoes
50 g/2 oz button mushrooms, wiped and halved or quartered
200 ml/7 fl oz tomato juice
1 tbsp freshly chopped basil
salt and freshly ground black pepper

Step-by-step guide

1 Deseed the peppers, remove the membrane with a small sharp knife and cut into small dice. Thickly slice the courgettes and cut the aubergine into small dice. Slice the onion into rings.

2 Place the tomatoes in boiling water until their skins begin to peel away.

3 Remove the skins from the tomatoes, cut into quarters and remove the seeds.

4 Place all the vegetables in a saucepan with the tomato juice and basil. Season to taste with salt and pepper.

5 Bring to the boil, cover and simmer for 15 minutes or until the vegetables are tender.

6 Remove the vegetables with a slotted spoon and arrange in a serving dish.

7 Bring the liquid in the pan to the boil and boil for 20 seconds until it is slightly thickened. Season the sauce to taste with salt and pepper.

8 Pass the sauce through a sieve to remove some of the seeds and pour over the vegetables. Serve the ratatouille hot or cold.

Marinated Lamb Chops with Garlic Fried Potatoes

Nutritional details

per 100 g

energy	177 kcals/744 kj
protein	10 g
carbohydrate	16 g
fat	9 g
fibre	1 g
sugar	0.4 g
sodium	trace

Ingredients — Serves 4

4 thick lamb chump chops
3 tbsp olive oil
550 g/1¼ lb potatoes, peeled and cut into 1 cm/½ inch dice
6 unpeeled garlic cloves
mixed salad or freshly cooked vegetables, to serve

For the marinade:

1 small bunch of fresh thyme, leaves removed
1 tbsp freshly chopped rosemary
1 tsp salt
2 garlic cloves, peeled and crushed
rind and juice of 1 lemon
2 tbsp olive oil

Step-by-step guide

1 Trim the chops of any excess fat, wipe with a clean, damp cloth and reserve. To make the marinade, using a pestle and mortar, pound the thyme leaves and rosemary with the salt until pulpy. Add the garlic and continue pounding until crushed. Stir in the lemon rind and juice and the olive oil.

2 Pour the marinade over the lamb chops, turning them until they are well coated. Cover lightly and leave to marinate in the refrigerator for about 1 hour.

3 Meanwhile, heat the oil in a large non-stick frying pan. Add the potatoes and garlic and cook over a low heat for about 20 minutes, stirring occasionally. Increase the heat and cook for a further 10–15 minutes until golden. Drain on absorbent kitchen paper and add salt to taste. Keep warm.

4 Heat a griddle pan until almost smoking. Add the lamb chops and cook for 3–4 minutes on each side until golden, but still pink in the middle. Serve with the potatoes, and either a mixed salad or freshly cooked vegetables.

cows' milk-free · egg-free · gluten-free · wheat-free · nut-free · vegetarian · vegan · seafood-free

Meatballs with Bean & Tomato Sauce

Nutritional details

per 100 g

energy	112 kcals/471 kj
protein	6 g
carbohydrate	12 g
fat	5 g
fibre	2 g
sugar	3 g
sodium	0.1 g

Ingredients **Serves 4**

1 large onion, peeled and finely chopped
1 red pepper, deseeded and chopped
1 tbsp freshly chopped oregano
½ tsp hot paprika
425 g can red kidney beans, drained
300 g/11 oz fresh beef mince
salt and freshly ground black pepper
4 tbsp sunflower oil
1 garlic clove, peeled and crushed
400 g can chopped tomatoes
1 tbsp freshly chopped coriander, to garnish
freshly cooked rice, to serve

Step-by-step guide

1 Make the meatballs by blending half the onion, half the red pepper, the oregano, the paprika and 350 g/12 oz of the kidney beans in a blender or food processor for a few seconds. Add the beef with some seasoning and blend until well mixed. Turn the mixture onto a lightly floured board and form into small balls.

2 Heat the wok, then add 2 tablespoons of the oil and, when hot, stir-fry the meatballs gently until well browned on all sides. Remove with a slotted spoon and keep warm.

3 Wipe the wok clean, then add the remaining oil and cook the remaining onion and pepper and the garlic for 3–4 minutes, until soft. Add the tomatoes, seasoning to taste and remaining kidney beans.

4 Return the meatballs to the wok, stir them into the sauce, then cover and simmer for 10 minutes. Sprinkle with the chopped coriander and serve immediately with the freshly cooked rice.

Mediterranean Rice Salad

Nutritional details

per 100 g

energy	48 kcals/202 kj
protein	1 g
carbohydrate	9 g
fat	1 g
fibre	trace
sugar	trace
sodium	trace

Ingredients Serves 4

250 g/9 oz Camargue red rice
2 sun-dried tomatoes, finely chopped
2 garlic cloves, peeled and finely chopped
4 tbsp oil from a jar of sun-dried tomatoes
2 tsp balsamic vinegar
2 tsp red wine vinegar
salt and freshly ground black pepper
1 red onion, peeled and thinly sliced
1 yellow pepper, quartered and deseeded
1 red pepper, quartered and deseeded
½ cucumber, peeled and diced
6 ripe plum tomatoes, cut into wedges
1 fennel bulb, halved and thinly sliced
fresh basil leaves, to garnish

Step-by-step guide

1. Cook the rice in a saucepan of lightly salted boiling water for 35–40 minutes, or until tender. Drain well and reserve.
2. Whisk the sun-dried tomatoes, garlic, oil and vinegars together in a small bowl or jug. Season to taste with salt and pepper. Put the red onion in a large bowl, pour over the dressing and leave to allow the flavours to develop.
3. Put the peppers, skin-side up, on a grill rack and cook under a preheated hot grill for 5–6 minutes, or until blackened and charred. Remove and place in a plastic bag. When cool enough to handle, peel off the skins and slice the peppers.
4. Add the peppers, cucumber, tomatoes, fennel and rice to the onions. Mix gently together to coat in the dressing. Cover and chill in the refrigerator for 30 minutes to allow the flavours to mingle.
5. Remove the salad from the refrigerator and leave to stand at room temperature for 20 minutes. Garnish with fresh basil leaves and serve.

✓ cows' milk-free ✓ egg-free ✓ gluten-free ✓ wheat-free ✓ nut-free ✓ vegetarian ✓ vegan ✓ seafood-free

Mushroom Stew

Nutritional details

per 100 g

energy	73 kcals/306 kj
protein	2 g
carbohydrate	13 g
fat	2 g
fibre	0.4 g
sugar	1 g
sodium	trace

Ingredients Serves 4

15 g/½ oz dried porcini mushrooms
900 g/2 lb assorted fresh mushrooms, wiped
2 tbsp good quality virgin olive oil
1 onion, peeled and finely chopped
2 garlic cloves, peeled and finely chopped
1 tbsp fresh thyme leaves
pinch of ground cloves
salt and freshly ground black pepper
700 g/1½ lb tomatoes, peeled, deseeded and chopped
225 g/8 oz instant polenta
600 ml/1 pint gluten-free vegetable stock
3 tbsp freshly chopped mixed herbs
sprigs of parsley, to garnish

Step-by-step guide

1 Soak the dried mushrooms in a small bowl of hot water for at least 20 minutes.

2 Drain, reserving the porcini mushrooms and their soaking liquid. Cut the fresh mushrooms in half and reserve.

3 In a saucepan, heat the oil and add the onion. Cook gently for 5–7 minutes until softened. Add the garlic, thyme and cloves and continue cooking for 2 minutes.

4 Add all the mushrooms and cook for 8–10 minutes until the mushrooms have softened, stirring often. Season to taste with salt and pepper and add the tomatoes and the reserved soaking liquid.

5 Simmer, partly covered, over a low heat for about 20 minutes until thickened. Adjust the seasoning to taste.

6 Meanwhile, cook the polenta according to the packet instructions using the vegetable stock. Stir in the herbs and divide between four dishes.

7 Ladle the mushrooms over the polenta, garnish with the parsley and serve immediately.

Orange Roasted Whole Chicken

Nutritional details

per 100 g

energy	223 kcals/933 kj
protein	20 g
carbohydrate	6 g
fat	13 g
fibre	0.2 g
sugar	5 g
sodium	0.1 g

Ingredients   Serves 6

1 small orange, thinly sliced
50 g/2 oz sugar
1.4 kg/3 lb oven-ready chicken
1 small bunch fresh coriander
1 small bunch fresh mint
2 tbsp olive oil
1 tsp Chinese five spice powder
½ tsp paprika
1 tsp fennel seeds, crushed
salt and freshly ground black pepper
sprigs of fresh coriander, to garnish
freshly cooked vegetables, to serve

Step-by-step guide

1 Preheat the oven to 190°C/375°F/Gas Mark 5, 10 minutes before cooking. Place the orange slices in a small saucepan, cover with water, bring to the boil, then simmer for 2 minutes and drain. Place the sugar in a clean saucepan with 150 ml/¼ pint fresh water. Stir over a low heat until the sugar dissolves, then bring to the boil, add the drained orange slices and simmer for 10 minutes. Remove from the heat and leave in the syrup until cold.

2 Remove any excess fat from inside the chicken. Starting at the neck end, carefully loosen the skin of the chicken over the breast and legs without tearing. Push the orange slices under the loosened skin with the coriander and mint.

3 Mix together the olive oil, Chinese five spice powder, paprika and crushed fennel seeds and season to taste with salt and pepper. Brush the chicken skin generously with this mixture. Transfer to a wire rack set over a roasting tin and roast in the preheated oven for 1½ hours, or until the juices run clear when a skewer is inserted into the thickest part of the thigh. Remove from the oven and leave to rest for 10 minutes. Garnish with sprigs of fresh coriander and serve with freshly cooked vegetables.

cows' milk-free · egg-free · gluten-free · wheat-free · nut-free · vegetarian · vegan · seafood-free

Oven-baked Pork Balls with Peppers

Nutritional details

per 100 g

energy	139 kcals/582 kj
protein	8 g
carbohydrate	5 g
fat	10 g
fibre	0.5 g
sugar	1 g
sodium	0.2 g

Ingredients Serves 4

450 g/1 lb fresh pork mince
4 tbsp freshly chopped basil
2 garlic cloves, peeled and chopped
3 sun-dried tomatoes, chopped
salt and freshly ground black pepper
3 tbsp olive oil
1 medium red pepper, deseeded and cut into chunks
1 medium green pepper, deseeded and cut into chunks
1 medium yellow pepper, deseeded and cut into chunks
225 g/8 oz cherry tomatoes
2 tbsp balsamic vinegar

Step-by-step guide

1. Preheat oven to 200°C/400°F/Gas Mark 6, 15 minutes before cooking.
2. Mix together the pork, basil, 1 chopped garlic clove, sun-dried tomatoes and seasoning until well combined.
3. With damp hands, divide the mixture into 16 equal portions, then roll into balls and reserve.
4. Spoon the olive oil into a large roasting tin and place in the preheated oven for about 3 minutes, until very hot.
5. Remove from the heat and stir in the pork balls, the remaining chopped garlic and peppers. Bake for about 15 minutes.
6. Remove from the oven and stir in the cherry tomatoes and season to taste with plenty of salt and pepper. Bake for about a further 20 minutes.
7. Remove the pork balls from the oven, stir in the vinegar and serve immediately.

Persian Chicken Pilaf

Nutritional details

per 100 g

energy	149 kcals/624 kj
protein	18 g
carbohydrate	12 g
fat	4 g
fibre	0.2 g
sugar	0.7 g
sodium	0.2 g

Ingredients Serves 4–6

2–3 tbsp vegetable oil
700 g/1½ lb boneless skinless chicken pieces (breast and thighs), cut into 2.5 cm/ 1 inch pieces
2 medium onions, peeled and coarsely chopped
1 tsp ground cumin
200 g/7 oz long-grain white rice
1 tbsp tomato purée
1 tsp saffron strands
salt and freshly ground black pepper
100 ml/3½ fl oz pomegranate juice
900 ml/1½ pints gluten-free chicken stock
125 g/4 oz ready-to-eat dried apricots or prunes, halved
2 tbsp raisins
2 tbsp freshly chopped mint
pomegranate seeds, to garnish

Step-by-step guide

1. Heat the oil in a large, heavy-based saucepan over a medium-high heat. Cook the chicken pieces in batches until lightly browned. Return all the browned chicken to the saucepan.

2. Add the onions to the saucepan, reduce the heat to medium and cook for 3–5 minutes, stirring frequently, until the onions begin to soften. Add the cumin and rice and stir to coat the rice. Cook for about 2 minutes until the rice is golden and translucent. Stir in the tomato purée and the saffron strands, then season to taste with salt and pepper.

3. Add the pomegranate juice and stock and bring to the boil, stirring once or twice. Add the apricots or prunes and raisins and stir gently. Reduce the heat to low and cook for 30 minutes until the chicken and rice are tender and the liquid is absorbed.

4. Turn into a shallow serving dish and sprinkle with the chopped mint. Serve immediately, garnished with pomegranate seeds, if using.

cows' milk-free · egg-free · gluten-free · wheat-free · nut-free · vegetarian · vegan · seafood-free

Pheasant with Sage & Blueberries

Nutritional details

per 100 g

energy	183 kcals/766 kj
protein	15 g
carbohydrate	9 g
fat	10 g
fibre	0.5 g
sugar	0.4 g
sodium	0.2 g

Ingredients Serves 4

3 tbsp olive oil
3 shallots, peeled and coarsely chopped
2 sprigs of fresh sage, coarsely chopped
1 bay leaf
1 lemon, halved
salt and freshly ground black pepper
2 pheasants or guinea fowl, rinsed and dried
125 g/4 oz blueberries
4 slices Parma ham or bacon
125 ml/4 fl oz vermouth or dry white wine
200 ml/⅓ pint gluten-free chicken stock
1 tbsp brandy
roast potatoes, to serve

Step-by-step guide

1 Preheat oven to 180°C/350°F/Gas Mark 4, 10 minutes before cooking. Place the oil, shallots, sage and bay leaf in a bowl, with the juice from the lemon halves. Season with salt and pepper. Tuck each of the squeezed lemon halves into the birds with 75 g/3 oz of the blueberries, then rub the birds with the marinade and leave for 2–3 hours, basting occasionally.

2 Remove the birds from the marinade and cover each with 2 slices of Parma ham. Tie the legs of each bird with string and place in a roasting tin. Pour over the marinade and add the vermouth. Roast in the preheated oven for 1 hour, or until tender and golden and the juices run clear when a thigh is pierced with a sharp knife or skewer.

3 Transfer to a warm serving plate, cover with tinfoil and discard the string. Skim off any surface fat from the tin and set over a medium-high heat.

4 Add the stock to the tin and bring to the boil, scraping any browned bits from the bottom. Boil until slightly reduced. Stir in the brandy and strain into a gravy jug. Add the remaining blueberries and keep warm.

5 Using a sharp carving knife, cut each of the birds in half and arrange on the plate with the crispy Parma ham. Serve immediately with roast potatoes and the gravy.

Poached Chicken with Salsa Verde Herb Sauce

Nutritional details

per 100 g

energy	182 kcals/764 kj
protein	25 g
carbohydrate	0.5 g
fat	9 g
fibre	0.1 g
sugar	0.2 g
sodium	0.2 g

Ingredients Serves 6

6 boneless chicken breasts, each about 175 g/6 oz
600 ml/1 pint gluten-free chicken stock, preferably homemade

For the salsa verde:
2 garlic cloves, peeled and chopped
4 tbsp freshly chopped parsley
3 tbsp freshly chopped mint
2 tsp capers
2 tbsp chopped gherkins (optional)
1 handful wild rocket leaves, chopped (optional)
2 tbsp lemon juice or red wine vinegar
125 ml/4 fl oz extra virgin olive oil
salt and freshly ground black pepper
sprigs of mint, to garnish
freshly cooked vegetables, to serve

Step-by-step guide

1 Place the chicken breasts with the stock in a large frying pan and bring to the boil. Reduce the heat and simmer for 10–15 minutes, or until cooked. Leave to cool in the stock.

2 To make the salsa verde, switch on the motor on a food processor, then drop in the garlic cloves and chop finely. Add the parsley and mint and, using the pulse button, pulse 2–3 times. Add the capers and, if using, add the gherkins and rocket. Pulse 2–3 times until the sauce is evenly textured.

3 With the machine still running, pour in the lemon juice or red wine vinegar, then add the olive oil in a slow, steady stream until the sauce is smooth. Season to taste with salt and pepper, then transfer to a large serving bowl and reserve.

4 Carve each chicken breast into thick slices and arrange on serving plates, fanning out the slices slightly. Spoon over a little of the salsa verde on to each chicken breast, garnish with sprigs of mint and serve immediately with freshly cooked vegetables.

cows' milk-free · egg-free · gluten-free · wheat-free · nut-free · vegetarian · vegan · seafood-free

Pork Cabbage Parcels

Nutritional details

per 100 g

energy	126 kcals/524 kj
protein	7 g
carbohydrate	6 g
fat	9 g
fibre	0.7 g
sugar	1 g
sodium	0.1 g

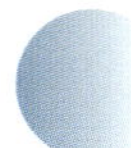

Ingredients Serves 4

8 large green cabbage leaves
1 tbsp vegetable oil
1 carrot, peeled and cut into matchsticks
125 g/4 oz fresh pork mince
50 g/2 oz button mushrooms, wiped and sliced
1 tsp Chinese five spice powder
50 g/2 oz cooked long-grain rice
juice of 1 lemon
150 ml/¼ pint gluten-free chicken stock

For the tomato sauce:
1 tbsp vegetable oil
1 bunch spring onions, trimmed and chopped
400 g can chopped tomatoes
1 tbsp freshly chopped mint
freshly ground black pepper

Step-by-step guide

1 Preheat the oven to 180°C/350°F/ Gas Mark 4, 10 minutes before cooking. To make the sauce, heat the oil in a heavy-based saucepan, add the spring onions and cook for 2 minutes or until softened.

2 Add the tomatoes and mint to the saucepan, bring to the boil, cover, then simmer for 10 minutes. Season to taste with pepper. Reheat when required.

3 Meanwhile, blanch the cabbage leaves in a large saucepan of lightly salted water for 3 minutes. Drain and refresh under cold running water. Pat dry with absorbent kitchen paper and reserve.

4 Heat the oil in a small saucepan, add the carrot and pork mince and cook for 3 minutes. Add the mushrooms and cook for 3 minutes. Stir in the Chinese five spice powder, rice and lemon juice and heat through.

5 Place some of the filling in the centre of each cabbage leaf and fold to enclose the filling. Place in a shallow ovenproof dish seam-side down. Pour over the stock and cook in the preheated oven for 30 minutes. Serve immediately with the reheated tomato sauce.

cows' milk-free · egg-free · gluten-free · wheat-free · nut-free · vegetarian · vegan · seafood-free

Roasted Lamb with Rosemary & Garlic

Nutritional details

per 100 g

energy	198 kcals/827 kj
protein	17 g
carbohydrate	9 g
fat	11 g
fibre	0.7 g
sugar	0.7 g
sodium	0.1 g

Ingredients Serves 6

1.6 kg/3½ lb leg of lamb
8 garlic cloves, peeled
few sprigs of fresh rosemary
salt and freshly ground black pepper
4 slices pancetta
4 tbsp olive oil
4 tbsp red wine vinegar
900 g/2 lb potatoes
1 large onion
sprigs of fresh rosemary, to garnish
freshly cooked ratatouille, to serve (see page 27)

Step-by-step guide

1 Preheat oven to 200°C/400°F/Gas Mark 6, 15 minutes before roasting. Wipe the leg of lamb with a clean damp cloth, then place the lamb in a large roasting tin. With a sharp knife, make small, deep incisions into the meat. Cut 2–3 garlic cloves into small slivers, then insert with a few small sprigs of rosemary into the lamb. Season to taste with salt and pepper and cover the lamb with the slices of pancetta.

2 Drizzle over 1 tablespoon of the olive oil and lay a few more rosemary sprigs across the lamb. Roast in the preheated oven for 30 minutes, then pour over the vinegar.

3 Peel the potatoes and cut into large cubes. Peel the onion and cut into thick wedges then thickly slice the remaining garlic. Arrange around the lamb. Pour the remaining olive oil over the potatoes, then reduce the oven temperature to 180°C/350°F/Gas Mark 4 and roast for a further 1 hour, or until the lamb is tender. Garnish with fresh sprigs of rosemary and serve immediately with the roast potatoes and ratatouille.

cows' milk-free · egg-free · gluten-free · wheat-free · nut-free · vegetarian · vegan · seafood-free

Sicilian Baked Aubergine

Nutritional details

per 100 g

energy	27 kcals/114 kj
protein	1 g
carbohydrate	4 g
fat	1 g
fibre	2 g
sugar	4 g
sodium	0.1 g

Ingredients Serves 4

1 large aubergine, trimmed
2 celery stalks, trimmed (optional)
4 large ripe tomatoes
1 tsp sunflower oil
2 shallots, peeled and finely chopped
1½ tsp tomato purée
25 g/1 oz green pitted olives
25 g/1 oz black pitted olives
salt and freshly ground black pepper
1 tbsp white wine vinegar
2 tsp caster sugar
1 tbsp freshly chopped basil, to garnish
mixed salad leaves, to serve

Step-by-step guide

1 Preheat the oven to 200°C/400°F/Gas Mark 6. Cut the aubergine into small cubes and place on an oiled baking tray.

2 Cover the tray with tinfoil and bake in the preheated oven for 15–20 minutes until soft. Reserve, to allow the aubergine to cool.

3 Place the celery (if using) and tomatoes in a large bowl and cover with boiling water.

4 Remove the tomatoes from the bowl when their skins begin to peel away. Remove the skins, then deseed and chop the flesh into small pieces.

5 If using, remove the celery from the bowl of water, finely chop and reserve.

6 Pour the vegetable oil into a non-stick saucepan, add the chopped shallots and fry gently for 2–3 minutes until soft. Add the celery, tomatoes, tomato purée and olives. Season to taste with salt and pepper.

7 Simmer gently for 3–4 minutes. Add the vinegar, sugar and cooled aubergine to the pan and heat gently for 2–3 minutes until all the ingredients are well blended. Reserve to allow the aubergine mixture to cool. When cool, garnish with the chopped basil and serve cold with salad leaves.

cows' milk-free · egg-free · gluten-free · wheat-free · nut-free · vegetarian · vegan · seafood-free

Spanish-style Pork Stew with Saffron Rice

Nutritional details

per 100 g

energy	144 kcals/602 kj
protein	11 g
carbohydrate	7 g
fat	8 g
fibre	0.3 g
sugar	0.4 g
sodium	0.2 g

Ingredients — Serves 4

2 tbsp olive oil
900 g/2 lb boneless pork shoulder, diced
1 large onion, peeled and sliced
2 garlic cloves, peeled and finely chopped
1 tbsp cornflour
450 g/1 lb plum tomatoes, peeled and chopped
175 ml/6 fl oz red wine
1 tbsp freshly chopped basil
1 green pepper, deseeded and sliced
50 g/2 oz pimento-stuffed olives, cut in half crossways
salt and freshly ground black pepper
fresh basil leaves, to garnish

For the saffron rice:

1 tbsp olive oil, 25 g
1 small onion, peeled and chopped
few strands of saffron, crushed
250 g/9 oz long-grain white rice
600 ml/1 pint gluten-free chicken stock

Step-by-step guide

1. Preheat the oven to 150°C/300°F/Gas Mark 2. Heat the oil in a large flameproof casserole dish and add the pork in batches. Fry over a high heat until browned. Transfer to a plate until all the pork is browned.

2. Lower the heat and add the onion to the casserole. Cook for a further 5 minutes until soft and starting to brown. Add the garlic and stir briefly before returning the pork to the casserole. Add the cornflour and stir.

3. Add the tomatoes. Gradually stir in the red wine and add the basil. Bring to simmering point and cover. Transfer the casserole to the lower part of the preheated oven and cook for 1½ hours. Stir in the green pepper and olives and cook for 30 minutes. Season to taste with salt and pepper.

4. Meanwhile, to make the saffron rice, heat the oil in a saucepan. Add the onion and cook for 5 minutes over a medium heat until softened. Add the saffron and rice and stir well. Add the stock, bring to the boil, cover and reduce the heat as low as possible. Cook for 15 minutes, covered, until the rice is tender and the stock is absorbed. Adjust the seasoning and serve with the stew, garnished with fresh basil.

✓ cows' milk-free ✓ egg-free ✓ gluten-free ✓ wheat-free ✓ nut-free ✓ vegetarian ✓ vegan ✓ seafood-free

Spiced Tomato Pilau

Nutritional details

per 100 g

energy	169 kcals/707 kj
protein	3 g
carbohydrate	31 g
fat	4 g
fibre	0.7 g
sugar	3 g
sodium	trace

Ingredients   Serves 2–3

225 g/8 oz basmati rice
1 tbsp olive oil
4 green cardamom pods
2 star anise
4 whole cloves
10 black peppercorns
5 cm/2 inch piece cinnamon stick
1 large red onion, peeled and finely sliced
175 g/6 oz canned chopped tomatoes
salt and freshly ground black pepper
sprigs of fresh coriander, to garnish

Step-by-step guide

1 Wash the rice in several changes of water until the water remains relatively clear. Drain the rice and cover with fresh water. Leave to soak for 30 minutes. Drain well and reserve.

2 Heat the oil in the wok, then add the cardamoms, star anise, cloves, black peppercorns and the cinnamon stick. Cook gently for 30 seconds. Increase the heat and add the onion. Stir-fry for 7–8 minutes until tender and starting to brown. Add the drained rice and cook a further 2–3 minutes.

3 Sieve the tomatoes and mix with sufficient warm water to make 450 ml/16 fl oz. Pour this into the wok, season to taste with salt and pepper and bring to the boil.

4 Cover, reduce the heat to very low and cook for 10 minutes. Remove the wok from the heat and leave covered for a further 10 minutes. Do not lift the lid during cooking or resting. Finally, uncover and mix well with a fork, heat for 1 minute, then garnish with the sprigs of fresh coriander and serve immediately.

cows' milk-free · egg-free · gluten-free · wheat-free · nut-free · vegetarian · vegan · seafood-free

Spring Vegetable & Herb Risotto

Nutritional details

per 100 g

energy	71 kcals/296 kj
protein	2 g
carbohydrate	9 g
fat	2 g
fibre	1 g
sugar	1 g
sodium	0.3 g

Ingredients Serves 4

1 litre/1¾ pint gluten-free vegetable stock
125 g/4 oz asparagus tips, trimmed
125 g/4 oz baby carrots, scrubbed
50 g/2 oz peas, fresh or frozen
50 g/2 oz fine French beans, trimmed
1 tbsp olive oil
1 onion, peeled and finely chopped
1 garlic clove, peeled and finely chopped
2 tsp freshly chopped thyme
225 g/8 oz risotto rice
150 ml/¼ pint white wine
1 tbsp each freshly chopped basil, chives and parsley
zest of ½ lemon
salt and freshly ground black pepper

Step-by-step guide

1 Bring the vegetable stock to the boil in a large saucepan and add the asparagus, baby carrots, peas and beans. Bring the stock back to the boil and remove the vegetables at once using a slotted spoon. Rinse under cold running water. Drain again and reserve. Keep the stock hot.

2 Heat the oil in a large deep frying pan and add the onion. Cook over a medium heat for 4–5 minutes until starting to brown. Add the garlic and thyme and cook for a further few seconds. Add the rice and stir well for a minute until the rice is hot and coated in oil.

3 Add the white wine and stir constantly until the wine is almost completely absorbed by the rice. Begin adding the stock a ladleful at a time, stirring well and waiting until the last ladleful has been absorbed before stirring in the next. Add the vegetables after using about half of the stock. Continue until all the stock is used. This will take 20–25 minutes. The rice and vegetables should both be tender.

4 Remove the pan from the heat. Stir in the herbs and lemon zest. Season to taste with salt and pepper and serve immediately.

cows' milk-free · egg-free · gluten-free · wheat-free · nut-free · vegetarian · vegan · seafood-free

Sweet Potato Crisps with Mango Salsa

Nutritional details

per 100 g

energy	141 kcals/582 kj
protein	1 g
carbohydrate	13 g
fat	10 g
fibre	0.5 g
sugar	0.2 g
sodium	0.2 g

Ingredients — Serves 6

For the salsa:

1 large, ripe mango, peeled, stoned and cut into small cubes
8 cherry tomatoes, quartered
½ cucumber, peeled if preferred and finely diced
1 red onion, peeled and finely chopped
pinch of sugar
1 red chilli, deseeded and finely chopped
2 tbsp rice vinegar
2 tbsp olive oil
grated rind and juice of 1 lime

450 g/1 lb sweet potatoes, peeled and thinly sliced
vegetable oil, for deep frying
sea salt
2 tbsp freshly chopped mint

Step-by-step guide

1 To make the salsa, mix the mango with the tomatoes, cucumber and onion. Add the sugar, chilli, vinegar, oil and the lime rind and juice. Mix together thoroughly, cover and leave for 45–50 minutes.

2 Soak the potatoes in cold water for 40 minutes to remove as much of the excess starch as possible. Drain and dry thoroughly in a clean tea towel, or absorbent kitchen paper.

3 Heat the oil to 190°C/375°F in a deep fryer. When at the correct temperature, place half the potatoes in the frying basket, then carefully lower the potatoes into the hot oil and cook for 4–5 minutes, or until they are golden brown, shaking the basket every minute so that they do not stick together.

4 Drain the potato crisps on absorbent kitchen paper, sprinkle with sea salt and place under a preheated moderate grill for a few seconds to dry out. Repeat with the remaining potatoes. Stir the mint into the salsa and serve with the potato crisps.

Venetian Herb Orzo

Nutritional details

per 100 g

energy	121 kcals/505 kj
protein	2 g
carbohydrate	17 g
fat	5 g
fibre	1 g
sugar	0.5 g
sodium	trace

Ingredients Serves 4–6

200 g/7 oz baby spinach leaves
150 g/5 oz rocket leaves
50 g/2 oz flat leaf parsley
6 spring onions, trimmed
few leaves of fresh mint
3 tbsp extra virgin olive oil, plus more if required
450 g/11 oz orzo
salt and freshly ground black pepper

Step-by-step guide

1 Rinse the spinach leaves in several changes of cold water and reserve. Finely chop the rocket leaves with the parsley and mint. Thinly slice the green of the spring onions.

2 Bring a large saucepan of water to the boil, add the spinach leaves, herbs and spring onions and cook for about 10 seconds. Remove and rinse under cold running water. Drain well and, using your hands, squeeze out all the excess moisture.

3 Place the spinach, herbs and spring onions in a food processor. Blend for 1 minute then, with the motor running, gradually pour in the olive oil until the sauce is well blended.

4 Meanwhile, bring a large pan of lightly salted water to a rolling boil. Add the pasta and cook according to the packet instructions, or until 'al dente'. Drain thoroughly and place in a large warmed bowl.

5 Add the spinach sauce to the orzo and stir lightly until the orzo is well coated. Stir in an extra tablespoon of olive oil if the mixture seems too thick. Season well with salt and pepper. Serve immediately on warmed plates or allow to cool to room temperature.

cows' milk-free · egg-free · gluten-free · wheat-free · nut-free · vegetarian · vegan · seafood-free

Warm Chicken & Potato Salad with Peas & Mint

Nutritional details

per 100 g

energy	138 kcals/577 kj
protein	12 g
carbohydrate	8 g
fat	7 g
fibre	1 g
sugar	1 g
sodium	trace

Ingredients Serves 4–6

450 g/1 lb new potatoes, peeled or scrubbed and cut into bite-sized pieces
salt and freshly ground black pepper
2 tbsp cider vinegar
175 g/6 oz frozen garden peas, thawed
1 small ripe avocado
4 cooked chicken breasts, about 450 g/1 lb in weight, skinned and diced
2 tbsp freshly chopped mint
2 heads Little Gem lettuce
fresh mint sprigs, to garnish

For the dressing:

2 tbsp raspberry or sherry vinegar
2 tsp gluten-free Dijon mustard
1 tsp clear honey
50 ml/2 fl oz sunflower oil
50 ml/2 fl oz extra virgin olive oil

Step-by-step guide

1 Cook the potatoes in lightly salted boiling water for 15 minutes, or until just tender when pierced with the tip of a sharp knife; do not overcook. Rinse under cold running water to cool slightly, then drain and turn into a large bowl. Sprinkle with the cider vinegar and toss gently.

2 Run the peas under hot water to ensure that they are thawed, pat dry with absorbent kitchen paper and add to the potatoes.

3 Cut the avocado in half lengthways and remove the stone. Peel and cut the avocado into cubes and add to the potatoes and peas. Add the chicken and stir together lightly.

4 To make the dressing, place all the ingredients in a screw-top jar with a little salt and pepper, and shake well to mix; add a little more oil if the flavour is too sharp. Pour over the salad and toss gently to coat. Sprinkle in half the mint and stir lightly.

5 Separate the lettuce leaves and spread onto a large shallow serving plate. Spoon the salad on top and sprinkle with the remaining mint. Garnish with mint sprigs and serve.

Warm Fruity Rice Salad

Nutritional details

per 100 g

energy	219 kcals/922 kj
protein	8 g
carbohydrate	38 g
fat	4 g
fibre	2 g
sugar	19 g
sodium	0.2 g

Ingredients   Serves 4

175 g/6 oz mixed basmati and wild rice
125 g/4 oz skinless chicken breast
300 ml/½ pint gluten-free chicken or vegetable stock
125 g/4 oz ready-to-eat dried apricots
125 g/4 oz ready-to-eat dried dates
3 sticks celery (optional)

For the dressing:
2 tbsp sunflower oil
1 tbsp white wine vinegar
4 tbsp lemon juice
1–2 tsp clear honey, warmed
1 tsp gluten-free Dijon mustard
freshly ground black pepper

To garnish:
6 spring onions
sprigs of fresh coriander

Step-by-step guide

1 Place the rice in a pan of boiling salted water and cook for 15–20 minutes or until tender. Rinse thoroughly with boiling water and reserve.

2 Meanwhile wipe the chicken and place in a shallow saucepan with the stock.

3 Bring to the boil, cover and simmer for about 15 minutes or until the chicken is cooked thoroughly and the juices run clear.

4 Leave the chicken in the stock until cool enough to handle, then cut into thin slices.

5 Chop the apricots and dates into small pieces. Peel any tough membranes from the outside of the celery (if using) and chop into cubes. Fold the apricots, dates, celery and sliced chicken into the warm rice.

6 Make the dressing by whisking all the ingredients together in a small bowl until mixed thoroughly. Pour 2–3 tablespoons over the rice and stir in gently and evenly. Serve the remaining dressing separately.

7 Trim and chop the spring onions. Sprinkle the spring onions over the top of the salad and garnish with the sprigs of coriander. Serve while still warm.

✓ cows' milk-free ✓ egg-free ✓ gluten-free ✓ wheat-free ✓ nut-free ✓ vegetarian ✓ vegan ✓ seafood-free

Warm Leek & Tomato Salad

Nutritional details

per 100 g

energy	66 kcals/277 kj
protein	2 g
carbohydrate	11 g
fat	2 g
fibre	1 g
sugar	6 g
sodium	0.2 g

Ingredients — Serves 4

450 g/1 lb trimmed baby leeks
225 g/8 oz ripe, but firm tomatoes
2 shallots, peeled and cut into thin wedges

For the honey and lime dressing:

2 tbsp clear honey
grated rind of 1 lime
4 tbsp lime juice
1 tbsp light olive oil
1 tsp gluten-free Dijon mustard
salt and freshly ground black pepper

To garnish:

freshly chopped tarragon
freshly chopped basil

Step-by-step guide

1. Trim the leeks so that they are all the same length. Place in a steamer over a pan of boiling water and steam for 8 minutes or until just tender.
2. Drain the leeks thoroughly and arrange in a shallow serving dish.
3. Make a cross in the top of the tomatoes, place in a bowl and cover them with boiling water until their skins start to peel away. Remove from the bowl and carefully remove the skins.
4. Cut the tomatoes into four and remove the seeds, then chop into small cubes. Spoon over the top of the leeks together with the shallots.
5. In a small bowl make the dressing by whisking the honey, lime rind, lime juice, olive oil, mustard and salt and pepper. Pour 3 tablespoons of the dressing over the leeks and tomatoes and garnish with the tarragon and basil. Serve while the leeks are still warm, with the remaining dressing served separately.

cows' milk-free · egg-free · gluten-free · wheat-free · nut-free · vegetarian · vegan · seafood-free

Wild Rice Dolmades

Nutritional details

per 100 g

energy	288 kcals/1187 kj
protein	3 g
carbohydrate	5 g
fat	29 g
fibre	0.8 g
sugar	0.4 g
sodium	0.4 g

Ingredients Serves 4–6

6 tbsp olive oil
25 g/1 oz pine nuts (optional)
175 g/6 oz mushrooms, wiped and finely chopped
4 spring onions, trimmed and finely chopped
1 garlic clove, peeled and crushed
50 g/2 oz cooked wild rice
2 tsp freshly chopped dill
2 tsp freshly chopped mint
salt and freshly ground black pepper
16–24 prepared medium vine leaves
about 300 ml/ ½ pint gluten-free vegetable stock

To garnish:
lemon wedges
sprigs of fresh dill

Step-by-step guide

1 If using the pine nuts, heat 1 tbsp of the oil in a frying pan and gently cook them for 2–3 minutes, stirring frequently, until golden. Remove from the pan and reserve.

2 Add 1½ tablespoons of oil to the pan and gently cook the mushrooms, spring onions and garlic for 7–8 minutes until very soft. Stir in the rice, herbs, salt and pepper.

3 Put a heaped teaspoon of stuffing in the centre of each leaf. If the leaves are small, put two together, overlapping slightly. Fold over the stalk end, then the sides and roll up to make a neat parcel.Continue until all the stuffing is used.

4 Arrange the stuffed vine leaves close together seam-side down in a large saucepan, drizzling each with a little of the remaining oil – there will be several layers. Pour over just enough stock to cover.

5 Put an inverted plate over the dolmades to stop them unrolling during cooking. Bring to the boil, then simmer very gently for 3 minutes. Cool in the saucepan.

6 Transfer the dolmades to a serving dish. Cover and chill in the refrigerator before serving. Sprinkle with the pine nuts and garnish with lemon and dill. **Please note that pine nuts should not be eaten by nut allergy sufferers.**

✓ cows' milk-free ✓ egg-free ✓ gluten-free ✓ wheat-free ✓ nut-free ✓ vegetarian ✓ vegan ✓ seafood-free